Coloring Celery

Published in the United States of America by Cherry Lake Publishing
Ann Arbor, Michigan
www.cherrylakepublishing.com

Reading Adviser: Marla Conn MS, Ed., Literacy specialist, Read-Ability, Inc.
Book Design: Jennifer Wahi
Illustrator: Jeff Bane

Library of Congress Cataloging-in-Publication Data

Names: Rowe, Brooke.
Title: Coloring celery / Brooke Rowe.
Description: Ann Arbor : Cherry Lake Publishing, 2017. | Series: My science
    fun | Audience: K to grade 3. | Includes bibliographical references and
    index.
Identifiers: LCCN 2016056317| ISBN 9781634728218 (hardcover) | ISBN
    9781634729994 (pbk.) | ISBN 9781634729109 (pdf) | ISBN 9781534100886
    (ebook)
Subjects: LCSH: Plants, Motion of fluids in--Juvenile literature. |
    Celery--Juvenile literature. | Vascular system of plants--Juvenile
    literature. | Food--Experiments--Juvenile literature.
Classification: LCC QK871 .R64 2017 | DDC 583/.9882--dc23
LC record available at https://lccn.loc.gov/2016056317

Printed in the United States of America
Corporate Graphics

About the illustrator: Jeff Bane and his two business partners own a studio along the American River in Folsom, California, home of the 1849 Gold Rush. When Jeff's not sketching or illustrating for clients, he's either swimming or kayaking in the river to relax.

Science Notes

Coloring Celery explores how plants obtain nutrients. In this experiment, the reader places a stalk of celery into water that has food coloring added. As the celery absorbs the water, the color spreads to the leaves.

Celery is a plant. Plants need water. It feeds them. The water travels to their leaves.

Look around. What plants can you find?

You can watch this happen.
How?

Let's find out!

- Food coloring (red or blue)

- Knife

- Vase of water

- **Stalk** of celery with leaves

You will need these things

Add a few drops of food coloring to the vase of water.

Ask an adult to help cut off the celery end that has no leaves. Put the stalk in the water.

13

Leave it there overnight. Check it in the morning.

Why do you think you
need to wait?

The leaves have turned the same color as the water.

Will green or yellow food coloring work?

Why or why not?

The celery drank the water.
It changed the leaves' color.

Try it with a bigger or smaller stalk of celery.

Try it with a flower!

Good job. You're done!
Science is fun!

What new questions do you have?

glossary

stalk (STAWK) the main stem of a plant from which the leaves and flowers grow

index